As You Like It

A Guide

by Alistair McCallum

Upstart Crow Publications

First published in 1996 by
Upstart Crow Publications

Reprinted 1997, 2004 and 2013

Copyright © Alistair McCallum 1996

A CIP catalogue record for this book
is available from the British Library

ISBN 978 1 899747 00 9

Printed in the UK by Berforts Information Press Ltd,
23 – 25 Gunnels Wood Park, Gunnels Wood Road,
Stevenage, Herts SG1 2BH

Upstart Crow Publications is a division of
The Language Studio Ltd
Berwick, East Sussex

www.shakespeare-handbooks.com

AS YOU LIKE IT: A GUIDE

The Shakespeare Handbooks

Available now:

- Antony & Cleopatra

- As You Like It

- Hamlet

- King Lear

- Macbeth

- A Midsummer Night's Dream

- Romeo & Juliet

- Twelfth Night

Forthcoming titles include:

- Othello

- Much Ado About Nothing

- The Tempest

The Shakespeare Handbooks are available at bookshops, or direct from the publisher at www.shakespeare-handbooks.com.

Setting the scene

Shakespeare wrote *As You Like It* in or around 1599, when he was in his mid-thirties. He was already a successful dramatist and actor, and a member – and shareholder – of the most prestigious theatre company in London.

His creative output at this time of his life was prolific and varied: *Much Ado About Nothing, Henry V, Julius Caesar, As You Like It* and *Hamlet* were probably all written within the space of two years. The other great tragedies, and the later, darker and more mysterious comedies, were yet to come.

Following its initial public performances at the Globe, and possibly some private performances for King James I a few years later, *As You Like It* was not played again for well over a hundred years. However, a revival at the Drury Lane theatre in London in 1740 – with actresses playing the female roles, rather than the boys of Shakespeare's time – proved an instant success. The play quickly became established as a perennial favourite, and has remained so ever since.

As You Like It, with its woodland setting, is frequently labelled a 'pastoral' comedy. But this suggests an idealised, sentimental view of life, and the play presents something much more subtle than this. Its pastoral stillness and simplicity is woven through with continual, lively threads of questioning, criticism, irony and discussion. Its enduring appeal lies in its thoughtfulness as well as in its delicate beauty.

"... the prose is light and sparkling and has the speed of talk as well as the form of art. The poetry has a lyrical clarity with overtones of gravity ... and the songs echo through the play with a grave sweetness. As a lyrical comedy of romantic love ... As You Like It stands supreme."

David Daiches, *A Critical History of English Literature*, 1960

Discord between brothers

Duke Frederick deposes Duke Senior ...

Duke Frederick has seized power. He has deposed his elder brother, Duke Senior, banished him and confiscated his lands.

The old Duke is now in exile, with a few followers, in the Forest of Arden.

The old Duke's daughter, Rosalind, has stayed behind at court to be with her beloved friend and cousin, Celia, daughter of Duke Frederick.

Oliver denies Orlando his inheritance ...

Sir Rowland de Boys, now dead, left most of his estate to his eldest son Oliver. In the will, he instructed Oliver to look after the education of the youngest son, Orlando.

Oliver, irrationally jealous of his younger brother, has refused to comply with his father's wishes. He has completely neglected Orlando's education, and refused even to hand over the thousand crowns left to Orlando in the will.

Curtain up

"The spirit of my father ..."

Orlando has reached the end of his tether. His anger against his older brother Oliver – who refuses to allow him a proper education – is overwhelming. With a good education, he could live up to his father's name: without it, he feels degraded and worthless.

When he sees Oliver, he finally boils over and attacks him. He demands the education due to him; or, at the very least, the thousand crowns left to him in the will. When Orlando finally lets go of him, Oliver half-heartedly promises that Orlando will get at least part of what he wants.

The scene is witnessed, mostly in unhappy silence, by old Adam. He was previously servant to Sir Rowland, whom he remembers with affection: he now serves Oliver, whom he can neither like nor respect.

As soon as Adam and Orlando have left, Oliver makes it plain that he has no intention of giving Orlando anything.

Charles is persuaded

Charles is the court wrestler, employed by Duke Frederick. He has a fearsome reputation, and takes on all comers in prize bouts.

He also has a sentimental, romantic streak, and talks wistfully of the exiled Duke Senior and his followers:

Charles: They say he is already in the Forest of Arden, and a many merry men with him; and there they live like the old Robin Hood of England. They say many young gentlemen flock to him every day, and fleet the time carelessly as they did in the golden world.

Charles has come to see Oliver because he is worried about a rumour that Orlando is to challenge him at the next wrestling bout. Presumably Orlando is keen to win the prize money, and prove his worth in the process.

"It is no laughing matter my friends, it is a weeping matter, a heavy matter, under the pretence for gathering for Robin Hood, a traitor, and a thief, to put out a preacher, to have his office less esteemed ... This realm hath been ill provided for, that it hath had such corrupt judgements in it, to prefer Robin Hood to God's word ..."

Bishop Hugh Latimer, 1549, complaining that festivities on Robin Hood's Day meant that no-one came to church.

As Charles says, he has a reputation to keep up: Orlando will not get special treatment, and is unlikely to escape without injury. Charles assumes, naturally, that Oliver will be concerned about his younger brother, and will try to dissuade him from fighting.

Oliver claims that he has tried, unsuccessfully, to do just that. But Orlando is stubborn; worse, he is ambitious and villainous: worse still, he is plotting against his own brother, Oliver: worst of all, he is plotting against Charles himself. If he does not defeat Charles in the wrestling,

> *Oliver:* ... he will practise against thee by poison, entrap thee by some treacherous device, and never leave thee till he hath ta'en thy life by some indirect means or other.

Even this, Oliver assures Charles, is putting it mildly:

> *Oliver:* I speak but brotherly of him ...

Charles believes every word without question. He leaves, determined to do his worst in the forthcoming bout. Oliver is confident that his problems with Orlando are over.

Rosalind and Celia

Rosalind is in low spirits. She misses her father, the banished Duke Senior. Celia tries to console her. She promises Rosalind that she will return all the lands confiscated by her father, Duke Frederick, when she inherits his estate.

They are talking of love, and the unfairness of life, when Touchstone, the court Fool, barges in. He is followed by Monsieur Le Beau, who manages to explain – after a barrage of teasing and interruptions – that the wrestling is about to take place. Charles is in good form, and has just defeated three opponents in a row, leaving a trail of pain and broken bones.

Rosalind is horrified. She cannot believe that anyone else will face Charles:

> *Rosalind:*   … is there any else longs to see this broken music in his sides? Is there yet another dotes upon rib-breaking?

They are unsure whether to stay and watch the wrestling, but it is too late. The contestants are already approaching. It is Orlando's turn.

A shock for Charles …

Duke Frederick leads the way. Even he is unhappy about the prospect of a contest between the hardened, brawny, aggressive Charles and the young, gentle opponent. He asks Celia and Rosalind to talk to the youth and persuade him to change his mind.

They try. Orlando is attentive and gracious, but firm in his intent. He has nothing to lose, he says; if he dies,

> *Orlando:*   I shall do my friends no wrong, for I have none
> to lament me; the world no injury, for in it I have
> nothing …

The fighting starts. To the delight of Rosalind and Celia, the young man seems to be getting the upper hand. As the wrestling goes on, the excitement rises. Orlando continues to resist Charles's onslaught, and refuses to be thrown.

There is uproar as, finally, Orlando throws Charles. Duke Frederick calls an immediate halt to the fight. The unfortunate Charles, unable to get up or even to speak, is carried out.

… and a shock for Orlando

It comes as an unpleasant surprise to Duke Frederick that the winner is a son of Sir Rowland de Boys. He was an enemy of Sir Rowland, although, as he admits, people in general held him in high esteem.

When the Duke leaves with his courtiers, the cousins stay behind to talk to Orlando. Rosalind remembers how her father, like everyone else, loved Sir Rowland, and she is horrified that she allowed his son to face the prize wrestler.

Rosalind, who was attracted to the young stranger as soon as he appeared, is rapidly falling in love with him, as he is with her. She gives him a chain from her neck, and is sorry that in her present state she has nothing more to offer:

> *Rosalind:*   Gentleman,
> Wear this for me; one out of suits with fortune,
> That could give more but that her hand lacks means.

Orlando is overcome with emotion and, like the defeated Charles, cannot speak. Rosalind persists, and before Celia manages to drag her away she makes her feelings clear:

> *Rosalind:*   Sir, you have wrestled well, and overthrown
> More than your enemies.

Orlando is left alone, overwhelmed by the passion that has suddenly come into his life.

Is it possible to judge, from his plays, what Shakespeare's personal beliefs and feelings were?

The scholar Caroline Spurgeon believed so, and, after a comprehensive analysis of Shakespeare's work, built up a detailed psychological profile of the man. Some of her conclusions seem particularly relevant to *As You Like It*:

"That which Shakespeare prizes most in life is unselfish love; what he instinctively believes to be the greatest evil is fear ... What most rouses his anger is hypocrisy and injustice, what he values supremely is kindliness and mercy."

Caroline Spurgeon, *Shakespeare's Imagery And What It Tells Us*, 1935

A discreet word from Monsieur Le Beau

One of Duke Frederick's courtiers, Monsieur Le Beau, comes back to speak unofficially with Orlando. His language is diplomatic, but his message is blunt. The Duke is displeased by the defeat of his wrestler at the hands of his old enemy's son. He is likely to behave irrationally: Orlando must escape immediately.

Monsieur Le Beau also reveals that the Duke is becoming more and more resentful of Rosalind. She has done nothing wrong, but is a constant reminder to everyone of the popularity of her father, the banished Duke Senior.

Orlando thanks Monsieur Le Beau for his advice, and sets off home.

Rosalind is banished   I, iii

Rosalind, lost in thought, is unwilling to talk. Celia tries to drag her out of her daydreaming, but it is not hard to see what is on her mind:

Celia: Come, come, wrestle with thy affections.
Rosalind: O they take the part of a better wrestler than myself.

As they discuss whether love at first sight is really possible, Duke Frederick enters.

Monsieur Le Beau was right. The Duke, tormented by jealousy, cannot stand the presence of Rosalind in his court any longer. Without any preliminaries, he announces that she is banished:

> *Duke Frederick:* Within these ten days if that thou be'st found
> So near our public court as twenty miles,
> Thou diest for it.

Rosalind is stunned. She asks what she has done to offend the Duke. Frederick at first accuses her of treason, but even he knows that she is innocent. Simply being the daughter of Duke Senior is enough.

Rosalind counters the Duke's accusations with forceful, reasoned argument, and Celia backs her up. The Duke refuses to listen. His obsession with unpopularity extends even to his daughter: he is convinced that people love Rosalind more than her.

> *Duke Frederick:* She is too subtle for thee, and her smoothness,
> Her very silence, and her patience
> Speak to the people and they pity her.
> ... she robs thee of thy name,
> And thou wilt show more bright and seem more virtuous
> When she is gone.

The Duke repeats his threat of death to Rosalind, and sweeps out with his courtiers. Rosalind and Celia remain, shocked, bewildered and alone.

An escape is planned

Soon the cousins' mood starts to brighten. Celia reassures Rosalind that she will not let her go into banishment alone; they will go together to the Forest of Arden and try to find the exiled Duke Senior.

For safety, they will change their courtly dress for old clothes. Rosalind decides to go even further, and disguise herself as a man. They choose new names to go with their new identities: Celia will call herself Aliena, while Rosalind, as a man, will become Ganymede. They decide to invite Touchstone, the court Fool, to join them.

They leave in high spirits, ready to collect together some jewels and valuables, find Touchstone, change their clothes and set off on their adventure.

> *"The play's title is not, perhaps, the throw-away phrase it may seem: during its course we see that the quality of human experience is influenced by the attitude that people bring to it."*
>
> Stanley Wells, *Shakespeare: A Dramatic Life*, 1994

As You Like It is set in France. The forest in which so much of the action takes place is, technically speaking, supposed to be the Ardennes forest in northern France, anglicised by Shakespeare to Arden.

However, the associations with Arden, a region in the rural heart of England, near Stratford-upon-Avon, are inescapable. Shakespeare's mother's family took its name from the area; her maiden name was Mary Arden.

"The main action of the play, then, takes place in a forest that he can only have associated, at every level, with his mother. In the symbolic language of all literatures and traditions, the Mother Forest is the wilderness that guards the mouth of the other world ..."

Ted Hughes, *Shakespeare and the Goddess of Complete Being*, 1992

In the Forest of Arden

Life is hard for the banished Duke Senior and his followers in Arden. There is no escape from the harshness of their surroundings, or the severity of the weather, and they must survive without any of the luxuries of the court.

Yet the old Duke remains optimistic. There is danger in the forest, he agrees, but it is preferable to the conspiracies of the court: and the cold wind may be cruel, but it enables him to understand and accept his own human frailty. Their life may be austere, but it is simple and satisfying:

> *Duke Senior:* Sweet are the uses of adversity ...
> And this our life, exempt from public haunt,
> Finds tongues in trees, books in the running brooks,
> Sermons in stones, and good in everything.

The Duke proposes that they go hunting for deer, though it grieves him that it should be necessary.

This point reminds them of Jaques, one of the Duke's followers, renowned for his melancholy and his love of argument. Jaques takes the side of the deer even more fervently than the Duke: at this very moment, they are told, he is holding forth on the wounded deer as a symbol of man's aggression and inhumanity. He is even suggesting that, by hunting the deer, Duke Senior's company are effectively doing what Duke Frederick did to them.

Duke Senior, positive as ever, is determined to enjoy the discussion, and they set off to find Jaques.

> "... the forest is an anarchist community run on the principle of co-operation between equals ... The myth behind this depiction is one dear to English hearts, of England as she was before foreign invasion brought kingship and barony ..."
>
> Germaine Greer, *Shakespeare*, 1986

Duke Frederick rages II, ii

Celia, Rosalind and Touchstone have set off for Arden. News of his daughter's disappearance reaches Frederick, who flies into a fury. He is convinced that his own followers are to blame; someone must have witnessed the flight and turned a blind eye. Those around him deny all knowledge of the escape, claiming that it must have taken place in the middle of the night.

It emerges that Celia's maid overheard the cousins praising Orlando after his victory in the wrestling. Duke Frederick immediately orders the arrest of Orlando, or – if he cannot be found – his brother Oliver.

Another shock for Orlando II, iii

Orlando has taken Monsieur Le Beau's advice, and has left the court. He is on his way back to his lodgings when he comes across Adam. The old man is beside himself with anxiety for the young Orlando, who reminds him so strongly of his old master Sir Rowland.

News of the wrestling has already reached Oliver. His plan to use Charles against his brother has failed: and Orlando's popularity, so maddening to Oliver, has risen even further. He has decided to take drastic action, and – as Adam has discovered – intends to burn down Orlando's lodgings this very night.

Orlando is faced with the prospect of a wandering, impoverished existence. At first, he decides that he would rather try to cope with his brother's constant malice. Then Adam reveals that, over the years, he has saved up some money to live on when he can no longer work. He will gladly give it all to Orlando, go with him as his servant, and leave Oliver.

Orlando is overjoyed, and accepts his offer with gratitude. The money is not much, but it should keep them in moderate comfort:

> *Orlando:*   ... we'll go along together,
> And ere we have thy youthful wages spent,
> We'll light upon some settled low content.

The two of them set off into the unknown.

Ganymede and Aliena find a home   II, iv

The three travellers have arrived in Arden: Rosalind (now dressed as a man and calling herself Ganymede), Celia (now Aliena, Ganymede's sister) and Touchstone. All three are exhausted and hungry. As they sit and rest, two shepherds appear.

"Shakespeare has no illusions; not even the illusion that one can live without illusions. He takes us into the Forest of Arden in order to show that one must try to escape, although there is no escape ..."

Jan Kott, *Shakespeare Our Contemporary*, 1965

Silvius, the younger, is hopelessly in love, and cannot stop talking about his adoration for the shepherdess Phebe. His companion Corin listens patiently: he has been in love himself in his youth. Suddenly Silvius rushes off, delirious with passion. Rosalind observes with sympathy: she has not forgotten Orlando. Touchstone recalls his own more homely experience of love:

> *Touchstone:* ... I broke my sword upon a stone, and bid him take that for coming a-night to Jane Smile; and I remember the kissing of her batler,[1] and the cow's dugs that her pretty chopt[2] hands had milked ...
>
> [1] *wooden bat for stirring laundry*
> [2] *chapped, scabby*

For the moment, Celia is more interested in food than love, and she gets the others to call the old shepherd over and ask for help.

It turns out that the shepherd's cottage, the sheep he tends and the land they graze on are all owned by Corin's master, not by the shepherd himself. As luck would have it, it is all for sale. Rosalind and Celia immediately offer to buy the property. They will live in the cottage, and Corin will be able to continue in his work as a shepherd.

Introducing Jaques

A few of Duke Senior's followers are gathered together, singing and chatting. Jaques effortlessly makes himself the centre of attention. He is proud of what he terms his 'melancholy', but his world-weary cynicism, and his ability to hold forth on any subject under the sun, tend to inspire affection rather than gloom.

When told that the Duke is looking for him, he answers, rather unconvincingly:

Jaques: ... I have been all this day to avoid him. He is too disputable for my company. I think of as many matters as he, but I give heaven thanks and make no boast of them.

> "... Jaques is the only purely contemplative character in Shakespeare. He thinks, and does nothing. His whole occupation is to amuse his mind, and he is totally regardless of his body and his fortunes. He is the prince of philosophical idlers; his only passion is thought ..."
>
> William Hazlitt, *Characters of Shakespeare's Plays*, 1817

More visitors to Arden II, vi

Orlando and Adam, fleeing from Oliver's hostile plans, have wandered unintentionally into the Forest of Arden.

Old Adam, weak with hunger, can go no further. Orlando reassures him that he will find some food, by hunting if necessary. He carries the old man to a sheltered spot, then sets out into the woodland.

A chance meeting in the forest ... II, vii

Duke Senior finally catches up with Jaques, who is almost speechless with laughter. While wandering through the forest, he has bumped into Touchstone, who has kept him amused for an hour with his attempts at philosophy:

> *Jaques:*   ... in his brain,
> Which is as dry as the remainder biscuit
> After a voyage, he hath strange places cramm'd
> With observation, the which he vents
> In mangled forms.

Jaques has developed a sudden fascination with foolery; he loves the idea of having the Fool's freedom to comment on all and sundry and to expose hypocrisy.

The Duke points out that, in court, Jaques was notorious for his debauchery and corruption, and is hardly the right person to criticise moral standards. Jaques brushes aside the objection and continues with his verbal onslaught.

... and another chance meeting

Orlando bursts onto the scene, sword drawn, demanding food.

Instead of the savagery he is prepared for, he is met with calmness and civility. He lays aside his sword and apologises; hunger had driven him to behave desperately.

He does not know who these forest dwellers are, and can only hope that they will take pity on him and Adam, and give them both food.

> *Orlando:*   ... whate'er you are
> That in this desert inaccessible
> Under the shade of melancholy boughs,
> Lose and neglect the creeping hours of time;
> If ever you have look'd on better days;
> If ever been where bells have knoll'd to church;
> If ever sat at any good man's feast;
> If ever from your eyelids wip'd a tear,
> And know what 'tis to pity and be pitied,
> Let gentleness my strong enforcement be ...

Duke Senior is moved. Without knowing it, the stranger has struck a chord with the Duke's own plight. Orlando is invited to join them. He accepts gratefully; but first he must return to find Adam and bring him to the banquet.

As You Like It was one of the first plays presented at the Globe Theatre, which was built in 1599 on the south bank of the Thames. Shakespeare was a member of the acting company – the Chamberlain's Men – which funded the new theatre. He had a 10% shareholding.

A painted sign outside the Globe showed Hercules carrying the world above his head. Beneath this picture was the theatre's Latin motto:

> *Totus Mundus Agit Histrionem*

In English, this translates, literally, as 'Everyone plays the player': 'Everyone acts a part': or, more elegantly,

> *All the world's a stage ...*

The seven ages of man

People should not dwell too much on their own unhappiness, observes Duke Senior:

Duke Senior: ... we are not all alone unhappy:
This wide and universal theatre
Presents more woeful pageants than the scene
Wherein we play in.

Jaques, always ready to pursue a philosophical argument, takes up the theme of the theatre:

Jaques: All the world's a stage,
And all the men and women merely players.
They have their exits and their entrances,
And one man in his time plays many parts,
His acts being seven ages.

He proceeds to deliver a bleak analysis of man's progress in life, from obnoxious childhood to discontented youth and self-satisfied middle age. The whole affair ends in senility:

Jaques:
>   Last scene of all,
> That ends this strange eventful history,
> Is second childishness and mere oblivion,
> Sans[1] teeth, sans eyes, sans taste, sans everything

[1] *without*

As if to illustrate this last age of man, the exhausted Adam is carried in by Orlando.

The feasting and music start again. The Duke is delighted to discover that the newcomer is a son of his beloved friend Sir Rowland de Boys, and welcomes him and Adam into his company.

"Nobody troubles to contradict his cynical Seven Ages of Man. The whole atmosphere of the place contradicts it."

Agnes Latham, Introduction to the Arden edition of *As You Like It*, 1975

Tradition has it that one of Shakespeare's younger brothers, who frequently went to London to see his big brother Will on the stage, became something of a celebrity in his old age, after Shakespeare's death. Actors and theatre buffs were keen to hear his memories of his famous brother.

As he grew older, his memory dimmed:

"... all that could be recollected from him of his brother Will, in that station was, the faint, general, and almost lost ideas he had of having once seen him act a part in one of his own comedies, wherein being to personate a decrepit old man, he wore a long beard, and appeared so weak and drooping and unable to walk, that he was forced to be supported and carried by another person to a table, at which he was seated among some company, who were eating, and one of them sang a song."

William Oldys, historian and collector, writing in the mid-18th century

If the story is true, then clearly Shakespeare had played the role of Adam in *As You Like It*.

Oliver is interrogated

Duke Frederick is in a vengeful frame of mind. Orlando, suspected of involvement in the disappearance of his daughter, is nowhere to be found. The Duke orders Oliver to find him and bring him back, dead or alive. If he fails to do so, his land and possessions will be seized by the Duke.

Frederick suspects that Oliver may have warned his brother to escape. Oliver's attempt to ingratiate himself with the Duke falls flat:

> *Oliver:*   O that your Highness knew my heart in this!
> I never lov'd my brother in my life.
> *Duke Frederick:* More villain thou.

Oliver is unceremoniously driven out of his house, and left to search for his brother.

The lover

Now that Orlando is freed from his immediate worries about food, shelter and safety, his thoughts return to Rosalind. He has written countless pages of love-poems, and is wandering around the forest fixing them to trees.

He opitomises Jaques' view of the third of the seven ages of man:

Jaques: ... the lover,
Sighing like furnace, with a woeful ballad
Made to his mistress' eyebrow.

"... the world of As You Like It *is still and golden, and most of its inhabitants would be content if some of its moments endured for ever ... it is the mellowest of Shakespeare's many worlds."*

Bertrand Evans, *Shakespeare's Comedies,* 1960

27

Sophistication *vs.* simplicity

Touchstone misses the court, and cannot raise much enthusiasm for the rustic life. He attempts to engage the old shepherd Corin in debate, but Corin is too straightforward for the Fool's meanderings.

As far as Corin is concerned, the court and country are different places with different customs, and he is happy where he is:

> Corin:　　　… I earn that I eat, get that I wear; owe no man hate, envy no man's happiness; glad of other men's good, content with my harm; and the greatest of my pride is to see my ewes graze and my lambs suck.

A 'touchstone' is a piece of hard, dark mineral used to test the quality of gold; when the metal is rubbed against the stone, the resulting mark indicates whether the gold is genuine or not.

"His name is not irrelevant, but his gibing wit, rather than proving the world of Arden false, proves it genuine."

Germaine Greer, *Shakespeare*, 1986

> *"... he is neither daunted with lightning and thunder, nor overjoyed with spring-time and harvest. His daily life is a delightful work, whatsoever the work be; whether to mend his garments, cure a diseased sheep, instruct his dog, or change pastures ... When he seems lazy and void of action, I dare approve his harmless negligence, rather than many approved men's diligence."*
>
> John Stephens, *Essayes and Characters: The Shepherd,* 1615

Rosalind learns of her admirer

Rosalind enters, reading aloud a verse that she has found fixed to a tree. She is followed shortly by Celia doing the same. Rosalind's surprise at seeing her name in the poems is outweighed by her dismay at the tediousness of the poetry.

However, her interest is aroused when Celia hints that she knows the identity of the author. Celia teases her with a few hints, and finally reveals the truth:

Celia: It is young Orlando, that tripped up the wrestler's heels and your heart, both in an instant.

Rosalind is staggered. Her first thought is the horrified realisation that she is disguised as a man: then a torrent of questions spills out. Before Celia has a chance to answer, Orlando himself comes into view.

Idealism *vs.* cynicism

Orlando, now staying with Duke Senior and his followers, has been walking with Jaques. The two do not get on.

Jaques:	I pray you mar no more trees with writing love-songs in their barks.
Orlando:	I pray you mar no more of my verses with reading them ill-favouredly.

Nevertheless, Jaques is curious about Orlando, and admires his quick answers. He invites Orlando to join him in conversation: but the offer is turned down by the idealistic Orlando, who is unimpressed by Jaques' talent for criticism.

In the safety of Arden, and the bliss of his love for Rosalind, Orlando has put his earlier tribulations behind him:

Jaques:	Will you sit down with me and we two will rail against our mistress the world and all our misery?
Orlando:	I will chide no breather[1] in the world but myself, against whom I know most faults.
Jaques:	The worst fault you have is to be in love.
Orlando:	'Tis a fault I will not change for your best virtue.

[1] *criticise no-one*

Jaques makes an ill-tempered exit.

A new friend for Orlando

Rosalind – now disguised as Ganymede, brother of the shepherdess Aliena – strikes up a conversation with Orlando. She is quick-witted, but has to keep up a constant struggle to hide both her femininity and her background. At times her guard slips:

Orlando: Where dwell you pretty youth?
Rosalind: With this shepherdess my sister; here in the skirts
  of the forest, like a fringe upon a petticoat.

Explaining his refined accent, Ganymede says that he was educated by an uncle who had lived at court. He switches instantly from court to courtship and love, which his uncle had strongly warned against. He mentions the poems that have been appearing on trees; whoever wrote those, he says, is suffering badly from love, and needs help.

Orlando confesses that he was the author. He does not look like a man in love, says Ganymede: he is not distracted and dishevelled, but disappointingly neat and tidy. Orlando insists passionately that his love is genuine:

Rosalind: But are you so much in love as your rhymes speak?
Orlando: Neither rhyme nor reason can express how much.

"Rosalind is the brightest of Shakespeare's bright heroines, and Orlando is the least conscious of his unconscious heroes. The gap between them is that between omniscience and oblivion."

Bertrand Evans, *Shakespeare's Comedies*, 1960

A cure for love

Ganymede says that he can cure Orlando of his love. This would involve daily visits to Ganymede, who would torment him by pretending to be Rosalind whilst behaving with wild unpredictability.

It has worked before, he claims:

Rosalind: … I drave my suitor from his mad humour of love
to a living humour of madness, which was, to
forswear the full stream of the world and to live in
a nook merely monastic. And thus I cured him …
Orlando: I would not be cured, youth.
Rosalind: I would cure you, if you would but call me Rosalind
and come every day to my cote and woo me.

Orlando has no intention of being cured of his love, but his curiosity gets the better of him and he agrees to go along with the game.

> "The heart of the comedy might be described as a demonstration of man's natural propensity for play."
>
> D. J. Palmer, *As You Like It and the Idea of Play*, 1971

Touchstone's wedding plans come to grief

Touchstone has decided to marry Audrey, a goat-herd living in the forest. In his own judgement, he is vastly superior to her in learning, culture and wit; he is nevertheless anxious for the wedding and its consummation.

He has found a village vicar who is prepared to marry them straight away, in the forest, without further ado. As far as Touchstone is concerned, the more informal the ceremony the better: the marriage will be that much easier to escape from in the future.

Jaques observes all this with disapproval, and refuses to take part. He tells Touchstone that he ought to go through a formal, proper ceremony:

> *Jaques:* Get you to church, and have a good priest that
> can tell you what marriage is. This fellow will but
> join you together as they join wainscot;[1] then one
> of you will prove a shrunk panel, and like green
> timber, warp …
>
> [1] *wooden wall panelling*

Touchstone reluctantly accepts his advice.

33

Unrequited love

Orlando is late for his visit to Ganymede. Rosalind is worried that he may prove just as unreliable in love, and is not encouraged by Celia's sceptical comments.

Rosalind mentions that she has met her father, Duke Senior, in the forest. He did not recognise her in her male disguise:

> *Rosalind:* He asked me of what parentage I was: I told him of as good as he ...

While they are waiting, Phebe enters, pursued by the young shepherd Silvius. Silvius is hopelessly in love with Phebe, but she rejects him: to make it worse, she refuses to show any sympathy for his suffering.

Rosalind, immediately taking the side of the love-sick shepherd, cannot resist joining the dispute. She scolds Phebe for her lack of compassion, tells her that she is a fool to reject the love of a good man, and makes a few insulting comments on her appearance into the bargain.

The speech does not have its intended effect. Phebe is charmed by the argumentative Ganymede:

> *Phebe:* Sweet youth, I pray you chide a year together.
> I had rather hear you chide than this man woo.

Rosalind tries to undo the damage she has done, but it is too late. She makes a hasty exit, leaving Phebe in a daze. The shepherdess realises that this is love:

> *Phebe:* Dead shepherd, now I find thy saw[1] of might,
> 'Who ever lov'd that lov'd not at first sight?'
>
> [1] *saying*

Phebe's quotation about love at first sight is from the unfinished lyric poem *Hero and Leander*. The 'dead shepherd' inevitably brings to mind its author, Christopher Marlowe, who had died, aged 29, some years before Shakespeare wrote *As You Like It*.

Marlowe, who was born in the same year as Shakespeare, had established himself in his short lifetime as one of the leading English dramatists. He had been a major influence on Shakespeare's work.

Phebe sends a letter

After the encounter with Ganymede, Phebe's feelings for Silvius seem to have undergone a sudden change. Although she still cannot love him, she now offers sympathy and even friendship. Silvius is overjoyed; an occasional smile from Phebe will be enough to keep his opirito up.

Phebe casually asks Silvius about Ganymede. She attempts to show a lack of interest in him, though her feelings get the better of her:

> *Phebe:* Think not I love him, though I ask for him.
> 'Tis but a peevish boy – yet he talks well –
> But what care I for words? Yet words do well
> When he that speaks them pleases those that hear.
> ... sure he's proud, and yet his pride becomes him.

She recalls the insulting comments that he made. She is so angry with him, she tells Silvius, that she is going to get her own back by writing a scathing letter in reply:

> *Phebe:* The matter's in my head, and in my heart.
> I will be bitter with him and passing short.

She has a favour to ask of Silvius: will he take the letter to Ganymede? The trusting, devoted Silvius consents at once.

Living in the present; a disagreement   IV, i

As Ganymede waits for Orlando's visit, Jaques holds forth on the pleasures of silence and melancholy.

In particular, he tells Ganymede, he enjoys reflecting nostalgically on his travels:

> *Jaques:* ... it is a melancholy of mine own, compounded of many simples,[1] extracted from many objects, and indeed the sundry contemplation of my travels, in which my often rumination wraps me in a most humorous sadness.
>
> [1] *basic ingredients*

Ganymede is sceptical about the virtues both of nostalgia and of travel:

> *Rosalind:* I had rather have a fool to make me merry than experience to make me sad, and to travel for it too!

He is suspicious of the motives of travellers. Do they travel because they are unable to feel at ease with their everyday surroundings – or even with themselves?

> *Rosalind:* Farewell Monsieur Traveller ... wear strange suits; disable all the benefits of your own country; be out of love with your nativity, and almost chide God for making you that countenance you are; or I will scarce think you have swam in a gondola.

"Foreign travel oftentimes makes many to wander from themselves as well as from their country ... and bring back less than they carried forth ... Nor can one hardly exchange three words with them at an ordinary* but presently they are th'other side of the sea, commending either the wines of France, the fruits of Italy, or the oil and salads of Spain."

* tavern

James Howell, *Instructions for Forreine Travell*, 1642

The love-cure continues

Orlando arrives. He is an hour late for his rendezvous with Ganymede, who scolds him, teases him and gets him to insist time and again on his love for Rosalind.

Ganymede calls Aliena over, and they go through a mock wedding ceremony. Ganymede assures Orlando that he will lose interest in Rosalind once they are married:

> *Rosalind:* No, no, Orlando, men are April when they woo, December when they wed.

As a wife, Rosalind will be demanding, difficult and changeable, claims Ganymede: but Orlando refuses to be discouraged.

Eventually Orlando has to go and join Duke Senior. He promises to be back later. Rosalind is more in love than ever.

A successful hunt IV, ii

Some of the Duke's followers have been hunting, and a deer has been killed. Jaques – despite his earlier claim to be on the side of the deer – is keen for the event to be celebrated in style. He singles out the successful hunter:

> *Jaques:* Let's present him to the Duke like a Roman conqueror; and it would do well to set the deer's horns upon his head for a branch of victory.

Boisterous singing and dancing follow, as the hunters make their way home.

A shock for Silvius ...

Orlando is late again. As Ganymede and Aliena wait, Silvius arrives with the letter from Phebe. He warns Ganymede that its contents are likely to be hurtful.

Ganymede looks at the letter and claims to be shocked by its spitefulness. However, as he reads it aloud it becomes impossible to hide the letter's true meaning. it is a declaration of Phebe's undying love for Ganymede. Silvius is distraught.

Ganymede is impatient with Silvius for continuing to love Phebe despite everything. However, he can see that Silvius is resolute, and tells him to take a message back to Phebe: that he will only consider her love if she will also find a place in her heart for Silvius.

Rosalind: ... go your way to her, for I see love hath made thee a tame snake, and say this to her: that if she love me, I charge her to love thee. If she will not, I will never have her ...

... and a shock for Rosalind

A stranger arrives, asking for directions to the farmhouse that Ganymede and Aliena have bought. It emerges that he is looking for Ganymede and Aliena themselves, and has been sent by Orlando, who has to miss the latest session of his love-cure. The stranger brings with him a bloodstained handkerchief.

He explains what has happened. Orlando had come across a man asleep under a tree. A lioness was watching over the man, ready to pounce as soon as he moved. Orlando realised that the sleeping man was Oliver, his murderous elder brother: nevertheless he attacked the lioness and scared her off, suffering a flesh wound in the struggle.

The stranger is none other than Orlando's brother Oliver, the man whose life Orlando has just saved. Thrown out of his house by Duke Frederick, he had come to Arden to find Orlando, capture him and return him, dead or alive, to the court. He has now repented, is happily reconciled with his brother, and has joined Duke Senior and his company.

Oliver used a handkerchief to bind the wound inflicted on his brother by the lioness. Orlando, now recovered, has asked Oliver to take the handkerchief to his friends to justify his absence. He hands it to Ganymede, who promptly faints.

Oliver reproaches the youth for fainting so easily. It was a sham, Ganymede assures him: he did it to demonstrate what Rosalind would have done. Ganymede and Aliena set off home, and Oliver goes back to join his brother.

Behind all the drama of the bloodstained handkerchief, another development has quietly unfolded. Love at first sight has struck again: this time the victims are Celia – in the guise of the shepherdess Aliena – and Oliver.

> *"Shakespeare is like a Bible; he creates his own myths. The Forest of Arden is a place in which all dreams meet; it is a dream and the awakening from a dream."*
>
> Jan Kott, *Shakespeare Our Contemporary*, 1965

Touchstone comes a step closer to marriage

Touchstone, dissuaded from Sir Oliver Martext's impromptu open-air wedding, has decided on a proper ceremony. There is one impediment: William, a local youth who is in love with Audrey.

Touchstone finds William and subjects him to a barrage of questions and mystifying comments. He informs William of his intention to marry Audrey, and orders him to give up any claim to her hand.

His threats are couched in scholarly terms, together with a translation for William's benefit:

> *Touchstone:* Therefore you clown, abandon – which is in the vulgar leave – the society – which in the boorish is company – of this female – which in the common is woman. Which together is, abandon the society of this female, or clown thou perishest; or to thy better understanding, diest; or, to wit, I kill thee …

The bemused William does as he is told.

The part of Touchstone was almost certainly written for the new 'clown' of Shakespeare's acting company, Robert Armin. Armin's style was worldly-wise, sophisticated and verbose; his predecessor, Will Kempe, had always relied more on crude, slapstick humour, and was notorious for his constant improvisation and interruption.

It is generally believed that Shakespeare and his colleagues were heartily relieved to be rid of Kempe when he left the company in 1599. Is it just coincidence that Audrey's slow-witted, tongue-tied admirer is given the name William?

"The other clown's name – William – is repeated three times, so that the audience will not miss the contrast between the departed company clown, William Kempe, and the new fool ... The traditional simple-minded rustic clown is symbolically dismissed from the new Globe stage."

David Wiles, *Shakespeare's Clown*, 1987

No more play-acting

The reconciled brothers are together again. The subject of their conversation is the irresistible attraction that overcame Oliver and Aliena on their first meeting.

Oliver intends to marry the shepherdess and give Orlando all the wealth that he had previously withheld from him, and much more:

> *Oliver:*   … my father's house and all the revenue that was old Sir Rowland's will I estate upon you, and here live and die a shepherd.

Ganymede enters. At first, the pretence that he is Orlando's beloved Rosalind continues: but Orlando is growing tired of the game. Now that Oliver is to be married, he misses the real Rosalind too painfully to joke about it.

Ganymede accepts this. The game is over, and he will no longer act the part of Orlando's sweetheart.

Ganymede's magical powers

Ganymede's tone becomes serious and intimate. He has something to confide to Orlando:

> *Rosalind:*   Believe then, if you please, that I can do strange things. I have since I was three year old conversed with a magician, most profound in his art and yet not damnable.

He can use his powers, he claims, to bring the real Rosalind into Orlando's presence. They can even be married along with Oliver and the shepherdess.

Orlando hardly dares believe him, but Ganymede insists:

> *Rosalind:*   ... put you in your best array, bid your friends; for
> if you will be married tomorrow, you shall; and to
> Rosalind if you will.

Promises

Phebe comes up to Ganymede, angry that he has revealed
the contents of her love-letter. Ganymede replies that he
has no intention of being considerate towards her as long
as she refuses to accept Silvius' love.

Phebe tells Silvius to explain how it feels to be in love.

> *Silvius:*   It is to be all made of sighs and tears,
>   And so am I for Phebe.
> *Phebe:*   And I for Ganymede.
> *Orlando:*   And I for Rosalind.
> *Rosalind:*   And I for no woman.

The declarations and accusations build up to a confused
crescendo, and Ganymede demands silence. He promises
that he will resolve everything:

> *Rosalind:*   [*To Phebe.*] I will marry you, if ever I marry woman,
>   and I'll be married tomorrow. [*To Orlando.*] I will
>   satisfy you, if ever I satisfied man, and you shall be
>   married tomorrow. [*To Silvius.*] I will content you,
>   if what pleases you contents you, and you shall be
>   married tomorrow.

They are all to meet together tomorrow, the date of Oliver's
wedding to Aliena.

A musical interlude

Tomorrow is also Audrey and Touchstone's wedding day. Audrey is eager to be married:

Audrey: I do desire it with all my heart; and I hope it is
no dishonest desire, to desire to be a woman of
the world.

Two of Duke Senior's pages join them, and launch into a song. The song includes an abundance of nonsense-words, but carries a clear theme: the beauty of love, youth and springtime, and the need to enjoy them while they last.

> And therefore take the present time,
>   With a hey and a ho and a hey nonino,
> For love is crowned with the prime,
>   In spring-time, the only pretty ring-time,[1]
> When birds do sing, hey ding a ding, ding,
> Sweet lovers love the spring.

[1] *time to exchange rings: time for wedding bells:
time for dancing*

As You Like It contains more songs than any other play by Shakespeare.

> "... in comedy he seems to repose, or to luxuriate, as in a mode
> of thinking congenial to his nature ... his tragedy seems to be
> skill, his comedy to be instinct."
>
> Samuel Johnson, Preface to his edition of the *Works of
> Shakespeare*, 1765

The big day arrives

V, iv

The Duke and his followers are gathered for the marriage
of Oliver and Aliena. Ganymede is present, as are the
other three whose marriages he has promised to bring
about: Orlando, Silvius and Phebe.

Ganymede reiterates the pledges that they have all made.
He is particularly keen to make sure that Phebe will agree
to marry Silvius if she changes her mind about Ganymede.
Her reluctance is matched by Silvius' zeal:

Rosalind:	But if you do refuse to marry me,
	You'll give yourself to this most faithful shepherd?
Phebe:	So is the bargain.
Rosalind:	You say that you'll have Phebe if she will?
Silvius:	Though[1] to have her and death were both one thing.

[1] *even if*

With a final reminder to all to keep their word, Ganymede
departs, along with his sister Aliena, to prepare the magical
transformation that will set everything right.

Touchstone gives a lesson in diplomacy

It is Touchstone and Audrey's wedding day too, and they turn up to join the ceremony. Jaques, now a firm friend of the Fool, introduces him to the Duke. Touchstone insists on his own credentials as a courtier:

> Touchstone: ... I have flattered a lady, I have been politic with my friend, smooth with mine enemy, I have undone three tailors, I have had four quarrels, and like[1] to have fought one.
>
> [1] came close

Jaques is keen to hear about the quarrel that nearly came to blows. The argument got as far as the seventh cause, explains Touchstone, mystifying his audience.

He patiently demonstrates the correct procedure for arguments between gentlemen:

> Touchstone: I did dislike the cut of a certain courtier's beard; he sent me word, if I said his beard was not well cut, he was in the mind it was; this is called the Retort Courteous. If I sent him word again, it was not well cut, he would send me word he cut it to please himself; this is called the Quip Modest ...

The dispute over the courtier's beard escalated, but not quite to the point of violence:

> Touchstone: I durst go no further than the Lie Circumstantial ... And so we measured swords and parted.

As Touchstone explains, he is a true courtier: he quarrels by the book.

Harmony

Ganymede has worked his magic. He has summoned up the god of marriage, Hymen, who joins the wedding celebrations. Hymen presents the Duke with his daughter Rosalind and his niece Celia. Ganymede and Aliena are nowhere to be seen.

The onlookers are dumbfounded. They can hardly believe their eyes:

Duke Senior: If there be truth in sight, you are my daughter.
Orlando: If there be truth in sight, you are my Rosalind.
Phebe: If sight and shape be true,
Why then my love adieu.

Under Hymen's direction, the four couples come together: Orlando and Rosalind –

Hymen: You and you no cross shall part.

Celia and Oliver –

You and you are heart in heart.

Phebe and Silvius –

You to his love must accord,
Or have a woman to your lord.

and Touchstone and Audrey.

You and you are sure together,
As the winter to foul weather.

As a solemn hymn to the honour of Hymen is sung, the wedding guests mingle, listening to each other's stories, piecing together the events that have led up to the present celebrations.

The restlessness, discontent and searching are at an end. The scene is suffused with love and reconciliation: even Phebe is happy with her Silvius.

A catastrophe is averted

A stranger bursts in. It is Jaques de Boys, second son of old Sir Rowland, brother of Orlando and Oliver. He brings news of Duke Frederick. It was Frederick who deposed the rightful ruler, his brother Duke Senior: and his jealous fury has also driven Rosalind, Celia, Orlando and Oliver into the forest.

Frederick has heard about the love and support inspired by the old Duke, even in exile. Burning with resentment, he has assembled an army, under his personal command, and marched on the forest, determined to kill his brother.

But Arden is full of surprises. When Frederick reached the forest, his life underwent a dramatic transformation:

> *Jaques de Boys:* ... to the skirts of this wild wood he came,
>   Where, meeting with an old religious man,
>   After some question with him, was converted
>   Both from his enterprise and from the world,
>   His crown bequeathing to his banish'd brother ...

Duke Senior is restored to power, and all the land and wealth confiscated from his followers is to be returned. The pastoral adventure is over: it is time to return to court.

Duke Senior: ... every of this happy number
That have endur'd shrewd[1] days and nights with us,
Shall share the good of our returned fortune ...

[1] *severe*

But for the moment, music, dancing and celebration are called for.

> "... the pastoral setting of sheep-cote and forest glade is not to be undervalued merely because the good characters leave it when their difficulties are resolved. For it is a healing place. Truth and recognition are to be found there ... the Duke and his companions have spent a fertile period of meditation and renewal. They have been in contact, for a time, with an older and simpler scheme of things."
>
> John Wain, *The Living World of Shakespeare*, 1964

Jaques goes in search of an argument

Jaques, ill at ease in the atmosphere of gaiety and harmony, decides to seek out the reformed Duke Frederick. The meeting will provide an opportunity for lengthy discussion and philosophising:

> *Jaques:*   Out of these convertites,
> There is much matter to be heard and learn'd.

He pays his respects to the newly-wedded couples, although he is less than optimistic about Touchstone's marriage:

> *Jaques:*   … And you to wrangling, for thy loving voyage
> Is but for two months victuall'd.

He makes a dignified exit.

The festivities begin

Love has carried the day: new life is in the air, and the future is bright.

As the dancing begins, and the drama draws to a close, Rosalind steps outside the play and invites us to share in its spirit.

———

Acknowledgements

The following publications have proved invaluable as sources of factual information and critical insight:

- David Daiches, *A Critical History of English Literature*, Secker and Warburg, 1960

- Bertrand Evans, *Shakespeare's Comedies*, Oxford University Press, 1960

- Germaine Greer, *Shakespeare*, from the *Past Masters* series, edited by Keith Thomas, Oxford University Press, 1986

- G. B. Harrison, *Introducing Shakespeare*, Pelican, 1966

- Ted Hughes, *Shakespeare and the Goddess of Complete Being*, Faber and Faber, 1992

- Jan Kott, *Shakespeare Our Contemporary*, Doubleday, 1965

- Agnes Latham, Introduction to the Arden edition of *As You Like It*, Methuen, 1975

- D. J. Palmer, *As You Like It and the Idea of Play*, from *Much Ado About Nothing and As You Like It: A Casebook*, edited by John Russell Brown, Macmillan, 1979

- Caroline Spurgeon, *Shakespeare's Imagery And What It Tells Us*, Cambridge University Press, 1935

- John Wain, *The Living World of Shakespeare: A Playgoer's Guide*, Macmillan, 1964

- Stanley Wells, *Shakespeare: A Dramatic Life*, Sinclair-Stevenson, 1994

- David Wiles, *Shakespeare's Clown: Actor and Text in the Elizabethan Playhouse*, Cambridge University Press, 1987

- John Dover Wilson, *Life in Shakespeare's England*, Cambridge University Press, 1911

All quotations from *As You Like It* are taken from the Arden Shakespeare.

You can order the *Shakespeare Handbooks*
direct from the publisher.

Visit: **www.shakespeare-handbooks.com**

Call: **01323 811187**

Free postage & packing in the UK.
Overseas customers please allow £1 per book.

———————————————

Titles currently available in the *Shakespeare Handbooks* series are:

❑ **Antony & Cleopatra** (ISBN 978 1 899747 02 3, £4.95)

❑ **As You Like It** (ISBN 978 1 899747 00 9, £4.95)

❑ **Hamlet** (ISBN 978 1 899747 07 8, £4.95)

❑ **King Lear** (ISBN 978 1 899747 03 0, £4.95)

❑ **Macbeth** (ISBN 978 1 899747 04 7, £4.95)

❑ **A Midsummer Night's Dream** (ISBN 978 1 899747 09 2, £4.95)

❑ **Romeo & Juliet** (ISBN 978 1 899747 10 8, £4.95)

❑ **Twelfth Night** (ISBN 978 1 899747 01 6, £4.95)

———————————————

Upstart Crow Publications will not pass your address on to other organisations.

Prices correct at time of going to press. Whilst every effort is made to keep prices low, Upstart Crow Publications reserves the right to show new retail prices on covers which may differ from those previously advertised in the text or elsewhere.